ACTION

BMX RACING

By K. A. Hale

Kaleidoscope

Minneapolis, MN

The Quest for Discovery Never Ends

This edition is co-published by agreement between
Kaleidoscope and World Book, Inc.

Kaleidoscope Publishing, Inc.
6012 Blue Circle Drive
Minnetonka, MN 55343 U.S.A.

World Book, Inc.
180 North LaSalle St., Suite 900
Chicago IL 60601 U.S.A.

Kaleidoscope ISBNs
978-1-64519-064-6 (library bound)
978-1-64494-145-4 (paperback)
978-1-64519-165-0 (ebook)

World Book ISBN
978-0-7166-4357-9 (library bound)

Library of Congress Control Number
2019904090

Printed in the United States of America.

Bigfoot lurks within
one of the images in
this book. It's up to
you to find him!

TABLE OF
CONTENTS

CHAPTER 1

PEDALING TO VICTORY

Priya rolls her BMX bike to the starting gate. She blocks out the cheering fans. She needs to focus. The gate drop is important. She wants to get the lead out of the gate. That could help her secure a win.

Getting out of the gate ahead of other riders gives BMX racers a great head start.

FUN FACT

A race sometimes only lasts for thirty seconds.

The gate is on top of a hill. It has eight lanes. It's a little taller than her bike's wheels. Her front wheel rests against the gate. The gate will drop when the race starts.

First, she has to get ready. Priya makes sure her bike is straight. Her hands are even on the handlebars. She keeps the **cranks** level. She puts her right foot on the pedal. Priya takes a deep breath. She needs to relax. If she is too stiff, she will tremble. Then it will be harder to balance. She puts her left foot on the pedal. She slowly stands up on the pedals. Her legs are bent slightly. Her wrists are pushed forward. She keeps her balance.

She hears the starting voice. "Riders ready. Watch the gate," it says. There's a loud beep. The gate drops. Priya is ready. She pushes her bike forward. She's the first one out of the gate. She pedals down the hill as fast as she can. She's faster than everyone else. She flies over the first jump. Then she speeds around the first turn. She's in the lead!

OBSTACLES

BMX tracks have different obstacles. A roller is one small hill. A double is two hills together. There's room in the middle to catch air. A step-up has two ramps. The second ramp is bigger. The tabletop is flat on top.

BMX riders need to practice good form so they can succeed in races.

There are obstacles ahead. She completes a step-up and a double. She turns again. Priya hears a clatter. Two riders have crashed. A third rider ran into them. Crashing is one danger in BMX racing. But Priya can't think about them. She has to keep going. She reaches the **rhythm section**. This section is different from others. She doesn't want to go high here.

Instead, she wants to have the best rhythm. She needs to know when to pedal and when to jump.

There's one more turn. Then there's a tabletop jump. She speeds past the finish line. Priya wins! She sees her parents cheering. Priya wants to race professionally someday. BMX racing is in the Olympics now. Maybe she will represent Team USA.

The rhythm section on a BMX racetrack is a series of small hills where riders try to get through quickly, rather than doing big jumps.

CHAPTER 2

BMX racing began when kids in California copied their favorite motocross racers on their bicycles.

FROM CALIFORNIA TO BEIJING

BMX racing began in the late 1960s. It started in California. **Motocross** racing was becoming popular. Kids would copy their favorite riders on their bicycles.

In 1971, Bruce Brown was making a movie. It was called *On Any Sunday.* The movie was about motocross racing. He saw some of the kids biking in California. He filmed them for his movie. People across the country watched. They learned about this new sport. At first, it was known as pedal-cross. Then it was called bicycle motocross. They called it BMX for short.

FUN FACT
No two BMX tracks are the same.

11

Bicycles cost less than motorcycles. People could afford to race. BMX became more and more popular. The first **sanctioning bodies** were founded in the 1970s. One was called the American Bicycle Association (ABA). The other was called the National Bicycle League (NBL). These organizations made sure races were fair.

BMX continued to grow. The International Cycling Union recognized BMX as an official cycling sport in 1993. This made BMX popular around the world.

BMX FREESTYLE

BMX racing is all about speed. But BMX freestyle is different. Freestylers focus on doing tricks. They try to get big air. Freestyle BMX was in the first X Games in 1995. The Olympic Committee made a big announcement in 2017. In 2020, Freestyle BMX would be included in the Olympics.

Many people like BMX racing.

13

BMX

RACING RECORDS

**Most Men's Olympic
Gold BMX medals**

Māris Štrombergs (Latvia)   2 medals

**Most Women's Olympic
Gold BMX medals**

Mariana Pajón (Colombia)   2 medals

**First Men's Olympic
Gold BMX medalist**

Māris Štrombergs (Latvia), 2008

**First Women's Olympic
Gold BMX medalist**

Anne-Marie Chausson (France), 2008

BMX took an even bigger leap in 2008. It went to China. BMX was included in the Olympics for the first time. It was held in Beijing, China. The world's best BMX racers competed.

The ABA bought the NBL in 2011. They became USA BMX. Now, all official tracks would follow the same rules.

People around the world watched the 2008 Olympics.

CHAPTER 3

BIKES, CLOTHES, AND GEAR

Jake has a long day ahead of him. He has a big BMX race today. His brother and sister will race, too. Their parents will cheer them on. Jake likes that the whole family can do BMX together.

Jake starts getting dressed. Riders have to be covered up for safety. Some wear short sleeves and shorts. But then they have to cover up with more gear. They wear elbow, shin, and knee pads. Jake wears long sleeves and pants.

FUN FACT

Some BMX races allow children as young as four years old to ride.

BMX racers have to wear protective gear like long sleeves and pants, gloves, and helmets.

He wore regular clothes when he first started riding. Now he has a special BMX outfit. His jersey has **mesh** panels on the side. It keeps him from getting too hot. The matching pants have kneepads built in. They'll help protect him if he falls. He wears skate shoes. They have flat bottoms. Older riders wear special shoes. They're designed for **clipless pedals**. But Jake's bike has **flat pedals**. Jake pulls on his gloves. He's almost ready to go.

Jake goes to the garage. He finds his helmet. Helmets are required for all riders. Most wear a full-face helmet like Jake's. It will protect his mouth and teeth if he falls. Jake also wears goggles. They keep the dirt out of his eyes.

Full-face helmets protect the mouth and teeth in case of a fall, and goggles protect a rider's eyes from dirt and dust that gets kicked up during the race.

THE BIKE

Handlebars

Brake lever

Front fork

Saddle

Crank Spokes

Wheel

Chain

Tire

Jake helps his parents load the bikes into the truck. He loves his bike. The frame is blue. It has yellow tires and handlebars.

BMX bikes can be customized in many different ways.

BMX bikes are different from road bikes. They are smaller and lighter. BMX riders stand on the pedals most of the time. That's why they keep the seat low. Road bikes have two brakes. But BMX riders only slow down at the finish line. They want to go as fast as possible during the race. They only need one brake. BMX bikes are also single speed. That means riders can't shift **gears**.

The bikes are secure in the truck. Jake and his family hop in. They can't wait to get to the track.

CHAPTER 4

RACING WITH THE PROS

Māris Štrombergs's father was the first person to take him to a BMX track. He was five years old. He cried. Everyone was bigger than him. The jumps were high. But he would come to love BMX. He would win the sport's first Olympic men's medal. Štrombergs is from Latvia. He won the gold medal at the 2008 Olympics. He defended his title at the Olympics in 2012.

Māris Štrombergs is known as "The Machine."

THREE STARS OF
BMX RACING

MĀRIS ŠTROMBERGS

Štrombergs was the first male Olympic gold medalist in BMX racing. He won in Beijing (2008) and London (2012). He is the only Latvian with two gold medals.

MARIANA PAJÓN

Pajón is a two-time Olympic gold medalist. She won in London (2012) and Rio de Janeiro (2016). She is only the second Colombian ever to win a gold medal in a summer Olympics.

CONNOR FIELDS

Fields, an American racer, won his first gold medal at the Rio de Janeiro Olympics in 2016. He has a strong online presence. He posts videos with tips for BMX riders.

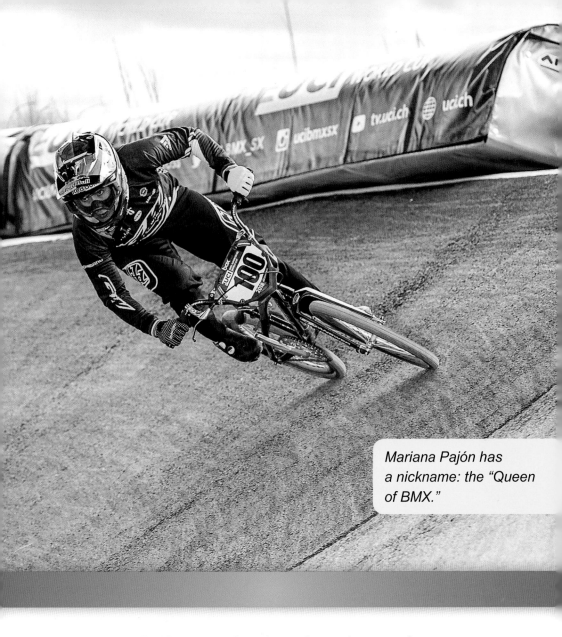

Mariana Pajón has a nickname: the "Queen of BMX."

Mariana Pajón started racing when she was four. She thought she'd go to the Olympics as a gymnast. But she found her fame as a BMX racer. Pajón won gold for Colombia twice. She won at the 2012 and 2016 Olympics. She has more Olympic gold medals than any female BMX rider.

American Connor Fields is another famous racer. In school, he won a geography bee. One answer was "Rio de Janeiro." That city would become very important. He would be a BMX racer in the Olympics there one day.

Fields came in seventh place at the London Olympics. He had to do better at the next one. It would be held in 2016 in Rio de Janeiro, Brazil. Fields broke his wrist early in the year. He wasn't sure he'd be able to compete. But he pushed through. He raced in the Rio Olympics. He won a gold medal.

Connor Fields is dedicated to BMX racing.

BEYOND

THE BOOK

After reading the book, it's time to think about what you learned.
Try the following exercises to jumpstart your ideas.

THINK

THAT'S NEWS TO ME. Think about the first-ever Olympic BMX race in Beijing. How might news articles give you more details about the race? What new information could you find in the articles? Where could you go to find those sources?

CREATE

PRIMARY SOURCES. A primary source is an original document created by someone who was at an event. These can include photographs, videos, or interviews. Make a list of different primary sources you might be able to find about BMX racing.

SHARE

SUM IT UP. Write one paragraph summarizing the important points from this book. Make sure it's in your own words. Don't just copy what is in the text. Share the paragraph with a classmate. Does the classmate have any comments about the summary or additional questions about BMX racing?

GROW

REAL-LIFE RESEARCH. What kinds of real-world places could you visit to learn more about BMX racing? What other topics could you explore there?

RESEARCH NINJA

Visit *www.ninjaresearcher.com/0646* to learn how to take your research skills and book report writing to the next level!

RESEARCH ....

DIGITAL LITERACY TOOLS

SEARCH LIKE A PRO
Learn about how to use search engines to find useful websites.

FACT OR FAKE?
Discover how you can tell a trusted website from an untrustworthy resource.

TEXT DETECTIVE
Explore how to zero in on the information you need most.

SHOW YOUR WORK
Research responsibly—learn how to cite sources.

WRITE ....

GET TO THE POINT
Learn how to express your main ideas.

PLAN OF ATTACK
Learn prewriting exercises and create an outline.

DOWNLOADABLE REPORT FORMS

FURTHER RESOURCES

BOOKS

Adamson, Thomas K. *BMX Racing*. Bellwether Media, 2016.

Hamilton, John. *BMX*. Abdo Publishing, 2015.

Omoth, Tyler. *First Source to BMX Racing*: *Rules, Equipment, and Key Riding Tips*. Capstone, 2018.

WEBSITES

FACTSURFER

Factsurfer.com gives you a safe, fun way to find more information.

1. Go to www.factsurfer.com.

2. Enter "BMX Racing" into the search box and click 🔍.

3. Select your book cover to see a list of related websites.

GLOSSARY

clipless pedals: Clipless pedals are bike pedals that connect to special shoes. Some riders prefer clipless pedals because they can go faster, but they can be dangerous if riders don't unclip when they fall.

cranks: The cranks are the part of the bike the pedals are on. The cranks should be level at the starting gate.

flat pedals: Flat pedals are bike pedals that can be used with any shoes. Most road bikes have flat pedals.

gears: A bike's gears change the difficulty of pedaling. BMX bikes are single speed and do not have different gears.

mesh: Mesh is a type of fabric with open holes. Jake's jersey has mesh fabric to keep him cool.

motocross: Motocross racing is motorcycle racing. Motocross racers use gas- or electric-powered motorcycles, while BMX bikes must be pedaled.

obstacles: Obstacles are things that get in the way or provide a challenge. Hills and turns are some of the obstacles in BMX racing.

rhythm section: The rhythm section is part of a BMX track with many small hills. To succeed in the rhythm section, riders need to know when to pedal and when to jump.

sanctioning bodies: The sanctioning bodies of sports set and enforce rules about a sport. The ABA was one of two sanctioning bodies for BMX racing before it bought the NBL.

INDEX

PHOTO CREDITS

The images in this book are reproduced through the courtesy of: MarcelClemens/Shutterstock Images, front cover (bikers); freelanceartist/Shutterstock Images, front cover (pattern); Adeline Helg/Shutterstock Images, front cover (dirt road); MarcelClemens/Shutterstock Images, pp. 3; homydesign/Shutterstock Images, pp. 4, 13 (top), 13 (bottom); Eric Buermeyer/Shutterstock Images, pp. 4–5; wayne midgley/Shutterstock Images, p. 7; StockphotoVideo/Shutterstock Images, pp. 8–9, 30; Galina Kovalenko/Shutterstock Images, pp. 10–11; Red Line Editorial, pp. 14, 24 (chart); Christophe Ena/AP Images, pp. 15, 24 (top); Robertomas/Shutterstock Images, pp. 16–17; Sergei Bachlakov/Shutterstock Images, pp. 18, 19, 22; ponsulak/iStockphoto, p. 20; skynavin/iStockphoto, p. 21; Sergey Ponomarev/AP Images, p. 23; Patrick Semansky/AP Images, p. 24 (middle); Pavel Golovkin/AP Images, p. 24 (bottom); Coudert/Sportsvision/Sipa/AP Images, p. 25; Carlos Herrera/Icon Sportswire/AP Images, pp. 26–27; A.Ricardo/Shutterstock Images, p. 27.

ABOUT THE AUTHOR

K. A. Hale is a writer and editor from Minnesota. She enjoys reading, writing, and playing with her dog.